T0351741

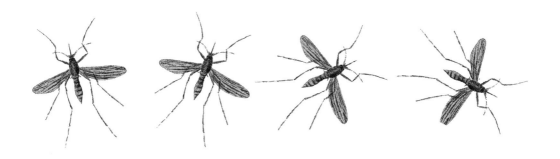

BROWNWOOD

LAWRENCE BRIDGES

T P

TUPELO PRESS
North Adams, Massachusetts

Library of Congress Cataloging-in-Publication Data available upon request.
ISBN: 978-1-936797-79-0

Cover and text designed by Howard Klein.

First paperback edition: April 2016.

Tupelo Press
P.O. Box 1767, North Adams, Massachusetts 01247
Telephone: (413) 664–9611 / editor@tupelopress.org / www.tupelopress.org

Tupelo Press is an award-winning independent literary press that publishes fine fiction, nonfiction, and poetry in books that are a joy to hold as well as read. Tupelo Press is a registered 501(c)(3) nonprofit organization, and we rely on public support to carry out our mission of publishing extraordinary work that may be outside the realm of the large commercial publishers. Financial donations are welcome and are tax deductible.

CONTENTS

FOREWORD

Who is Brownwood?

Brownwood, like Berryman's Henry, is a triad (I, He, You) "other" character. Camus once said, "He who despairs of the human condition is a coward, but he who has hope for it is a fool." Accidentally enlightened, Brownwood is both coward and fool, declaring: "The music I distrust stirs my inner fool." Lawrence Bridges's third book is a series of monologue-like entries that reveal an autobiography of someone stuck inside the vessel of who he is, yet very much part of the outside world in a malevolent mix of hope and despair. "Feared as a monster, tame as a clown," Brownwood is a dolphin man, a clock, a tree surgeon, mumbler, lover, inventor, office worker, writer, outlaw, failure, father, and one-as-many; this fictionalized character is an outsider longing to connect with himself: the persona / protagonist diminished by complacency (the world's and his own). But he's a flawed, disillusioned stand-in for himself, and perhaps for our disaffected generation defined by the intimate anonymity afforded through social media. Brownwood's character is irreverent, full of angst, wry humor, and sarcasm; he's a lost twin, a doppelgänger living in a melancholy place of indeterminacy, ultimately memorialized by his faltering behaviors.

This book's poetic plot (and subplot figuration) arrives with cinematographic aplomb. The visual narrative shots add up to scenes; scenes add up to sequences; sequences add up to the "wake parade" that is Brownwood. Yet the book's prose-like fragments (jazz riffs, journal entries, statements of address) follow an elliptical order. Brownwood's wayward logic contains the strange-mundane and a delightful, unpredictable specificity. Like consciousness itself, its radical shifts and movements, its strophic and antistrophic play become the formatting equivalence of survival. Brownwood survives a fall from grace through the imagination. He affirms his own imagination as a necessity, his method for processing bleak reality. Brownwood also escapes the dry simulation of reason by using deadpan humor, espousing philosophical capitulation, and changing the rules of fate and folly. "Caution says stop yourself," but he doesn't—he won't, because comfort comes in as an amalgam of absurdities: real and imagined.

"From space, the world looks free from regret." From Brownwood's vantage point, there's just "some road, both directions a puzzlement." So Brownwood struggles through a Dante's Inferno–type journey, ascending and descending the spiritual transcendence of "normal life" where "The Nightlight's Like a Welder's Spark" and "Confession Is a Plate" of gluttony and limbo. This fun, absurdist story follows a colloquy of crises measured by a future, though inevitable, that never comes. Body is time, body is place, and place is Brownwood's time-scape. Like the body, "Time is decline," yet Brownwood remains grounded in the present-tense real-life geography of recurrence, renewal, and surprise, as witnessed here:

A SPY ON A DESTRUCTIVE CHASE, YOUR CAR, ONE OF TWENTY REBOUNDS

> The world renews itself this way forever. This house will be
> leaving the world. I stop the alarm clock before it rings. I run
> my finger along the grout and trace a trolley route of those who died
> not yet fully traveled. The calendar of courage called my week.
> It's going to be a beautiful day. I'm going to be doing this for a long
> time, pushing three kinds of trash cans: good, bad, and green.

Even ennui and melancholy become part of Brownwood's defiance of time, of his battle with insignificance and extinction. He can claim any discomfort as a choice ("I'm going to be doing this for a long time"), a triumph of barbarity. Brownwood's obsession, his juxtapositional mockery of time, reveals a lively argument for existence that, by natural default of association with the everyday "good, bad, and green," therefore becomes ours too. Repeat after me: I am Brownwood, and "So the argument goes . . . The part of me you see is here."

Elena Karina Byrne

UNDERTOW

This hand's shadow plays over the page. I drag my left hand against it—
This hand moves down music, the memory of sex, darker flowers, over
riverbed of green, over things unsaid concealed in song, allowing
no reply, like a light left on all week. A bird lands on the fountain.
I build it a wing. I make something simple, then rest in the winging-it-
heart. I confess in the only language I know, building new wing versions
on the way down. The music I distrust stirs my inner fool.

THAT I'M A MAMMAL, TOO

He's talking to me. Preparing something someone won't read four hours
from now. I'm talking software and fall into an empty mood, if that's what
I'm looking at when I see unfinished things. I might just know where I am.
To him, my figure disappears; he sees my fool or a hotel clerk gone to barking.
It fritters me like bee noise, empty hives pulled to town for the pollinated.
He is speaking. Like a park ranger, he catches me running from a wilderness
when I'm angry that I have a sexual desire that possesses me.

MAN IN TAN PASSING ME ON THE LEFT

Running, carry-ons swaying, banging my knees. The eye (I lost an eye)
is morning from black to gray to blue. I'm awake. I walk through a spider
web in a dark driveway, which was the sign most of us were looking for.
My coat is missing. I have no arm and there's my mitt. I wonder at hands.
My ears are gone too. I will hear you without a body. I still hear the lazy
clanging of a railway crossing, the clicking of a slow train moving lumber
south. Birds piece it together for me. Music teachers owe so much to birds.

I MET AN ACROBAT WHO SAID THIS PLACE HAD A NASTY ROOM ROLL

The body got colder. The weather remained the same.
"I'm fond of you," I said, but nobody bought the irony or
would answer. "Stop whistling, you wind," he said, late
in the snow day, "I'm going to find out you are a dump truck."
It's camp for nausea, the wind-swinging kind.
If I could just wander home to my dirt floor.

HAUNTING THE YARD

How great the grandiose dream still is: You feel it hoisting
you into a side-yard tree to look for the source of the music.
A blank expression crosses your face. Then the morning moon again
bleeds white, changing to washed day, like an unexpected parting.
The moon marks our ancient folly, ruled by happenstance.
There you are in the sun, bedclothes hanging, moths and insects
roaring around in a miniature, big-city skin.

THE SUCCESSFUL CAPITALIST KNOWS THIS

There's a clean quiet of idle road maps, of cliffs minus bulldozers
cleaning messes, a streetlight in another time zone, waiting for eyes
to speed around a corner. The mind may feel fine, except for panic.
My legs, detached, walked old routes through broken rooms. Didn't
you know? The dancing fruit fly has, at its center, medical DNA as
it leaps and tickles the keyboard as if inspired. Sometimes a cold wind,
sub-rosa, sub-silence, or mere mute hearing tackles the problem of passing time
and confirms its smoothness. Yes, even the heart beats moments before failure.

THE DRY WIND IN COALINGA MADE ME CRAVE ALMONDS

A deep ravine where shouts engineer a crossing, simmering
winter scenes, strokes of action, eyes peering below ice,
surprised by photos of First Ladies floating at the bottom . . .
Our house floats in a pageant of chores and makes new ruts in
the prairie. Now I'm counting, now reminiscing, now despairing,
over what? I smile at that: If people were gardens, I'd be a birdbath
and a cactus, my mission abandoned.

CONFESSION IS A PLATE

on which you ride to the table of your own gluttony.
The distant lights of squid fisheries way out in the bay,
an owl's whimper after feast of other bird, chocolate on
my fingers, buffalo meat on a lower shelf in the freezer,
fried bananas in every smell, fennel tea in a wake-parade,
wishbones from the gory pile, and a muffin to keep in my
briefcase—a broken cereal bowl with a heart at the bottom.
Not hungry, little cabbages twirling, yourself saying goodbye.

RETREATING TO OUR FAVORITE SPOT FOR DINNER

You'd find mice and spiders, the burning cinches and tack,
palliating, faking famine, tears for all who walk away with
their jokes, smokeless, before alarm-time. Christopher Walken.
With copy and cant that whizzed by, so go the hours, brought
into the 'hood, the timescape when you wouldn't brood, but
sang, another seeker broken whole from sleep, with good news
against a body failing to catch its breath. "Sorry."

A HEAD OF LETTUCE IS STUCK IN THE AIR SHAFT

The shaky old scarecrow came with its smile across a stubble field.
Each rising took me farther from the start of this. You feel the floor
beneath your shoes, a lavender of owl's clover, the wind of swift
justice. In a heavy-gravity corridor, this desert had the lungs to blow
down trucks. I didn't get up early to suffer, to whine back with
the doves' falsetto plea. The dog barked all night at something
invisible. It's better to be insane and do the thinking.

THE USES OF HANDS

I wake with window eyes and a slickness of hair. The plowing
of bodies went as planned, but the fields fled and left us rocks,
stone henges to fertility and moon science. Blame light sorrow for this
dawn of icy wind. Then the markets react to the news, blight farms till all
eyes are cameras, with the tents and herds gone on, forgotten like an oral
tradition. History has taken itself with it. I'm fine, dressed as a carpenter,
too drugged to fly. The families are pluck and nothing gives to eat.

POLLINATED INTO A FERTILE ORCHARD

You know the rules: weightless, mad song, memory of birth.
Waves roll in unanimously. Faces stroll, side by side. I begin a story
that speeds then slows—more than my mind plays out on that field.
Sleep takes me to the past: war and a future, inside the eddy of a flute.
Dressed in new museums, customs, and slang, the unrinsed count
the germs that linger in smoke. So, how do you know?
Loaded into your own body, you are exhausting the original.

THE PROP MAN THOUGHT THE GUN WAS FAKE

I ran for sheriff. I reached for a large book on a tribe,
the night wreckage of a possum, the years after lost years,
tales of ambition, emotion, and love, everything in retrospect,
the unprotected who flee winter, ants that carry a deliverance
of twigs . . . to get myself on the leafy sidewalk. You see:
My condition befitted a cult for all citizen audiences.

THE FLU SNIFFLE MISTAKEN FOR A VELCRO RIP

Everyone wakes to the same shocking letdown. The police
don't even notice you as they scan for unknowable profiles.
This is the restaurant where we waited for the Kennedys, when you
stood in formal dress, in a place of kissing hello. You pass a friend's
house, she with the newly broken heart, and think it will heal, and then
you pass this way again. You'd rather be another person, headache
hibernating in a pain-killed spring dream. You say I clap my hands once,
leave the house, and point when I'm happy.

I WAKE, A HYBRID

I don't want to know about other lives today. The merciful earth heaves
again as it dries, while mosquitoes angle up and down all day to be born in
the standing pool. The orange groves of my youth, the dark orange sky,
a comic's landscape shoved to the eyes like a postcard with oranges . . . He didn't
get what he got by simmering like a teapot. His orange period. I see his thumb
from midcentury smoothing the mortar between bricks. All these walls
and not a thumb remains. My fingers smooth the air.

THE SEA IS CLOSE BUT WE NEVER GO THERE

I press my face to glass, call it time, the present, a sheet of wind I make
heading toward forgetting, a holiday where I'll start each phrase with "the."
Not because they're organized down the beach highway, but because
I'm spilled. Ghosts of future ghosts meet here in these field afternoons,
make deadline near the body of a comatose dog.

THIS ACT THAT BRINGS YOU THROUGH DOORS

The sky is like a tired body. I'm standing, throwing weightless hours
at the moon, watching it finish its business with the earth's shadow.
The front door opens to a crowd rushing in from the dark morning
on a lane of slippery blossoms. Time is decline. At the conclusion
I'll give myself ample warning, when that skein of sadness that impairs
sight becomes permanent. I'll snap from obsolescence and glimpse
at the infinite, and leave with a map. To see if I can leave myself:
I'll recall the door I came from was next to the door I entered.

GROWN TOO LARGE FOR HIS DOOR

The Dutch side decimated by age and accident—someone's large
rubber cables twist over the patio, and we've lived here while all this
went on. We're not the last survivors. Faces stream by, crossing
the yard and down into the canyon for cross-examinations and
for arming semantic traps. I'm trained to ignore them, but I'm shy.
I'm lost, arguing for the tenth time that the filing away of my feet
doesn't exceed my growth in height. Justice is just a toy.

YOU PULL ON A SLEEVE AND SHRINK

Your body is about wreckage of the weekend. You wake traffic lights
that have talked to themselves all night. Teenagers coast into driveways all
over town, engines cut. The turn-offs back up with morning drivers. Your
tone changes when you speak. You have one memory left of this place. Your
foot shrinks as your heart enlarges. Packed the cars and, back home, back
East, they stare at you like a primitive emerging from the woods, a lost
settler. The gullies are quiet and you're dressed in a wet sheet.

THE MAN IN A STARCHED SUIT DOING SERVICE

The reflecting vest of a garbage man in the black morning's headlights
looks like jeweled royalty in the street. The skinny man in sweaters
eyes the patrol car, blinking. Cool man, the passenger, heard something
fall in the night. Lake, ice, frozen man, sun, rocks, cascade, air, way out
of my range, a fish man (as I too ride) wears sorority shoes. A visionary
holds court in a corner. A crooked man stands atop a turtleback. Habit man
withholds the truth. We slowed, but the mystery car did not overtake us.

I SPEAK SOMEWHAT INCONVENIENTLY

in pajama bottoms, in townhouses in the discarded city, on
feet that cheat in shoes not sized for thick socks, in restaurants, on
sand with waves crashing, in a crowd, in half, in an open studio
unhappy by choice, in a compound, pooling for weeks with fish friends
breeding, in the pretty squeaks of a lonely neighbor's yard, in the basement
of the old hospital, in lucky talk time, marched in like a backward giraffe,
in the motionless drawer, in a deserted hotel, in a time of relief,
postwar, in entitled years, in hope for my survival.

THEIR SON WAKES UP IN FAR—AWAY PHOENIX AND THROWS ALL DOUBTS ASIDE

It is mid-day and you're stopping traffic of hill-bound trucks.
You get over-talked by a colleague. You have the time, picking palettes
from clown ears, easels from knees of audiences hungry with walla for
something to start. And you, with bed sheets still white from youth,
open like shop doors at nine. The crosswalks sizzle with candies
sewn to the feet of the walk of the satisfied girls who peer beyond
for catastrophe or money, and you, filled by sight . . . not ever there,
which flows from running as fast as you can, now skiing, now
gunning the V-8. Breathe in this rich arsenal of self and time.
Not all time (your small science kit) is vapor now.

IN THE MIDDLE OF THE NIGHT: CAR ALARM

Each day begins with the end of days in mind, the body ticking
giddy for rhythm; your bed, a desk, and plants coming out of the wall
like pictures. You turn and look down a straightaway toward the village:
All greens with no obstacle, like a big rock fallen on ants. Time is short
to ride decay into decay. This is the part of the brain never to be used again.
From space, the world looks free from regret.

THE BOXES WILL BURN

Just play the beauty box and never trust sleep again. Without a body, you're all
errands and speed and truculence and the unnecessary courtship in it. Flying,
depending on which direction you view evolution, like chimney wisps floating
straight up in the cold morning, glowing, fires in fifty-gallon drums, unbathed
people, anarchy, but no murder yet, where you will start and end at the least motel.
Wake it, unlock the house, roam, juggling these parks for fading vocabularies of
aroma, pleasure, then beauty. Life is a string or, worse, a quick squiggle.

FERAL CAT TAKING EXCEPTION

The celebrity snapped this picture that made the papers, paparazzi
tackled the kid who fled, and the diplomat from south of here,
held at gunpoint by his teenager, lived. While others flew past
various hysterias, you grew stones. Now it's fashionable to push
them around town in strollers. Our guide apologized for the trucker
jargon. I gulped, cleaned a nail, and noted that my hands, in their
precision, made up for my sloppiness of speech and absence
of gravitas. A wave sent a thump, mistaken for a quake.

THE FISH KIDS TOTE POPCORN THE SIZE OF PUNCHING BAGS

How much tissue do I throw away when I sneeze?
Smell is like this. The dead sense sniffs. Such is color now,
the French curve. They'll never catch you. They scream across
the open country, and his life accelerates to a higher bet.
Stop me. I have absolutely nothing to do. I ignore faces. I had
this feeling, strolling on bones. Yup. This miser heel keeps a skeletal
bar, serves ribbons of spirits that twist to the floor.

SOMETHING'S WALKING ON THE ROOF NOW

A secret art propagates through pictures of sounds. Erasers smooch pages
to lighten the overdraw, to subtract and baffle with modernist code. Thanks
for letting me borrow it with the location map and wet pages of a travel book.
My galoshes tell the story, wading about in sopped socks, miles of trip wires
behind me, neighbor's turkey chirping. And ho!, the dead silence heading east.
How nice the blood, how thorough the symphony before starting, the buckling
sound, tourettesing quips beyond the range of your instrument.

I WORRY THAT YOU ARE ORDINARY

Earthquake is my mind. I cough twice, lightly, sitting
on a one-legged stool so I won't doze off while assembling
explosives for avalanches. I'm willing to thaw my effigy
from droughts of decades past. The winter says goodbye
in gibberish, greasy and dark, with my eccentric renegade smile.
It's normal to feel this way in a town of artists all correcting each other.

ALACRITY AT MIDNIGHT

When it's July and undeserved, I gape at my wife and tell her I can
get nothing more done. That's poetry, this isn't? A full-bodied bear
sniffed our window—then there was heartbreak as if lasting a thousand
years, knowing of the cures on the way from space-medicine and renewal
of the world. You're a toy in a plastic box (months creep up in boxes) in
the Midwest, a coyote crying for help in the early dark, this stormy jade
in a vast square. You're textless, silent. *One mind at a time* is my motto.

FOLLOWED

The rest is messiness getting worse . . . like bedtime relief, like
the crisp boost, circles and ponds, like a bubble blown while setting
to serve, butterflies framed, sight like a lifelong sadness,
like blood in plastic, thinking a twin language, like all the phones
ringing at once, wetsuits like beetles sunning the arctic dusk, hours within days,
or the storms that have murdered our weather, like a numbed back nerve,
a fish floating in the air-as-water, like me, it can't stand more than a day off
per month, like an oral tradition ready for a meal by suture-light.

LISSETTE DIED SEWING

I walked in the dark through a beaded web a spider made
while I slept. I thought I fell asleep in a theater and the film
startled me awake, or I was awake and the film surprised me,
or I was thinking of a film when the web touched my face, or
it was like a film when I battled the web away from my face and
my hair in the dark, Van Gogh–moon and spider down my back.

SHE TALKS, HE TALKS

She sat on concrete, talking gravely. She talked at home, looked down
from a window, paced with heart in half, answered his gaze with silent words,
as if it were *she* looking at *him,* straight-on. She drives and speaks,
almost laughs, as she turns. He speaks scooters. She pauses and thinks
of her life with all of her men dead. He dries himself, admires his hair—
sea with woodcut waves. He fits into a shoe and falls back short another day.
They are on vacation together, married, kids hiking: nearby lake, speckle of
sunlight. Meadow stream. Sad eddy. Simple dam.

THE CUP WAS UPSIDE DOWN AND WHITE

It's a fixed egg and brittle . . .
You look down the boulevard, whitened.
A child hops crosswalk stripes, holding a hand.
Two headlights this morning in the dark lingered
like snakebite, white dots, no blood. Youth
is dead. Caution says stop yourself.

IMPROMPTU INTERVIEW

I'm not a musician, always stopping to listen to myself.
I'm not invited to this session with cool smokers who croon
in one room with candles. Music again: when branches fall
to kill, where whales breed, in the church, music's stern factory.
Here come the gulls and *their* music, in a liquid architecture, in a small
tropical shrub, in the wrong gender. All the friends who call me best friend
are coming over, unshaven, from the sliver chill and sand pelting,
outstretched arms with coffee cups. I make an appearance with a prop
plane. I live in a shadow house up the street, but don't tell.

ALL HAVE THE SAME BIOLOGY AND VIOLINS

For this you're never prepared: tourist birds and a hovering sense
that love lasts when bones shoot sideways. The flowers this season
stand in the raw path of anguished police enforcing the positive law.
Nice people ask you to putt and end with a round of horseshoes.
Hurrahs from dodgeball fill the park beneath white park light.
The trace of hail that bleached the rails and shoos away storms
melted from sight like a permanent sadness. Tall old friends holding
glasses notice you at the door, bewildered, at the wrong house.

I FEEL LIKE THE SPANISH WORD FOR TUNA

A stack of magazines, a wooden vent cap tapping in a frigid breeze.
Dust floats in shafts of winter light through splintered timbers
that cross you daily while the light moves north and human breath
mutters south. It is where you live, inside your meal, thumb pressed
to the frame of your head, fingers in the act of gathering skin, as if
pulling a brain string. You return to no road and no parking space,
your car parked in another neighborhood.

I'D MADE IT PAST SQUAD CARS

That patch of ground you call a garden, the contraption in the garage
you call a new career, and that marble thing in the front yard you
call Fred . . . You're so entertained indoors now, you never leave, you
stand between two cars in the driveway, a national pastime. The sprinkler
along the sidewalk breaks at its base and lifts a fountain, automatically.
A bugle. In color code not intending to imitate stars, I'll sit on my lawn
and sink like the fountain into a soft dimple of grass. I'll stand outside
with neighbors who, themselves, will betray you by dying or moving.

THE MP'S HOLSTER WAS EMPTY

Our pals saved the day. Our pals moved past military sentries
with clay characters. I was another one with the T-shirt I slept in this
early morning. We moved the Gross National Product down the road.
Our pals saved the day by hitting the lights. I go there, but there are no
lights. I'm blind, looking in on a fool's game in the rumble of blown
Chevys. I'm founding a theater today: "Stages of Last Resort."

EVERYTHING ALWAYS WAS

Fix a button in the dark. Relax and feel for the tracks as if you
were a small train. Now it's working, you dressed to let someone go.
You're moving to keep things efficient, where thought moves on heart
feet. Move the camp on. With your attitude of nothing-to-prove in a time
of rescue, you just dream now. Now, orange sky. Now, circuit breaker,
skin flakes. Now, to errands all night in animal weight. Do not take
comfort in the night, darker now as you cross town, people fighting.
You're an "other" to survivors of Spanish massacres, long ago.

YES NO FLIP—FLOPS

Let's get started. Don't record this. We'll receive a lei from a smiling
flower-crowned island girl, buxom with leis for others. We'll end up
at the gym under a podcast. We'll thank everyone who helped. Throw me
the phone. A sharp pencil will nick my wrist, trying to catch it as it falls
off the desk. A legitimizing self-consciousness now makes me your instant
friend, hours away. I think I see Africa or China. The phone wants to go off
just like Wagner. Yes, no one remembers nothing happens. The adults
seem not to care who was there first.

TWO MORNINGS: NOVEMBER

If I'd looked around the corner, I'd have seen myself.
I think: "Every morning's rising in the dark, rises *from* it not *to* it."
Here, plates clang for breakfast, and the snow-capped wall rises
into blue. A welt with a mouth and a voice grows on this irritated
thumb, demanding pencil, plank, and sight on this paint-splattered
hand. *All these years clear-headed with dark clouds approaching.* I think,
"I'll be lost in the gully of my thirst." My agent would have said,
"Better to be delusional about your simplicity in a grandiose world."

WITH NO SHIRT FOR THE INTERVIEW

You sleep in a wagon with a lover. When you wake, you just throw up
her long white dress, then shave under a tree, juggle in the next town,
and eat berries from the mountain. This is a day when it's not cold
by the banks next to a deeper wilderness with killer men about.
You're a relentless or an idiot-wanderer seeking relief from torment
at midnight, dragging a plasma drip, banging on factory doors,
feared as a monster, but tame as a clown with stiff missing fingers.

IT'S BETTER WET IN YOUR HEAD

Across the sprayed patio and wet deck chairs I smell the fresh stale
smell of flatwork steaming, everything turned off and the city below
with points of light, the shape of a flood plain. Our talk was repetition,
occult wheezing, a word or two forward each time, fast enough to crack
ceramic. A woman, ten years into the future, waves from a planet
with a note in her hand. In the present she is popular, unwrecked.
Meet here forever. Neither of us is afraid. Subtract that.

WE'RE ON A CELESTIAL RIDE

The journey most days is over my head, as is the sky,
the cosmos. I've been to the Very Large Array. We are
to the radio-scopes as ants are to sprinklers. Styrofoam packing-
nuggets quaver on the sand like a thousand ancestors, troubling.
The world changed while I've been standing here, not me. A dawn
of circles ascends through clouds. In dreaming you were elsewhere.
Don't you think our solar system hung the bed sheets out to dry?

I HAVE MY SEX IN SOMEONE

The loose captions for cups that ride the shelf of the bored-of-Christmas
wrestlers, big babies who gamble, rustics and whining cat, mothers who
puff stogies and fathers who burn bags of cash on a day for feet. She swings
and grazes windows down a street. "The bends!" The shelf in the air
is tilted up. My feet kick up a fan of water, my upper arm rolls the Ferris
wheel of the lazy pier. A rocky naked world is better than a repeating one.

I ROSE ACCUSING MYSELF

Open the windows and fly through nothing. Either way you're not
in New York, or Paris, looking at people passing. Far is Moscow,
Santiago, Perth. Houses in all directions become mountain ranges,
landscapes where no plan reprieves me. I hear a generation of
the highly skilled walking dead propped against months of scuppers
dripping or thermoses sipped while catching fish.
I should be rewarded in skates. There's only one direction.
The present is an edge of a circle expanding.

AT FIRST, BUT ACTUALLY

It's a quaint town where Europeans speak Valley Speak and show no
misunderstanding. A truck's coughing is purring. Have a drink
with the Thursday-night crowd, see some pretty girls, the white goose
I once kept. It's a holiday. It occurred to me (feather begging a hand to touch)
it works this way. I've made tools, quantum garage tools. I started to believe
who sews, sews instances, more lost than the worst of them. Forbearance
rules. Our marshals kiss mold off wrappers between shifts.

NIGHT ROAD

The town square is a hospital for those not speaking.
A village floated out to suicide, as swiftly as the fog carried
in smells of shoreline. We pulled the body from the gravitation of
logic, and this went on every quarter mile. It is you driving,
and this ends our road show. You're in this empty hall of encores.
You create a second act lasting twenty-five years, fifteen when you
think about it, because the last ten are for consequences.

ONE COULD JUST STOP AND NOT BE NOTICED

The deer, the fox, the mouse, the puma, the bobcat, the owl, the hawk,
the rattlesnake, the coyote, the possum—and the rabbit works without
caution. The ceiling twists like somebody's screwing a bottle cap on tight.
The news said storms, biblical storms: another turn on the clovered
freeway. I stop in the alley with the long blue fence where the carnival
parks its rides before setting up. A cut-out raccoon walks the wall at night
to drink the run-off. There's only one direction a sane person can look.

FOR MOMENTS LIKE THIS

The car covered in leaves rolled along with the traffic
like a wedding coach. The trees wanted a wedding. The rural
thicket spread, and you chewed—a dandy rainbow dug an end
into Alcatraz and you snapped, the wrong map in your packet.
Deaf among redwoods, this isn't how you saw this shape:
the skeleton of the man, all the leaves fallen with hues.
It takes sun, play, display of skin. No more. Never merry.

FALSE SUMMER: A STORY

Fatigued, I pulled over and took a nap by the graveyard.
The day was gone early, just afternoon—the dead had
accomplished more by lying there—and later that evening,
at the wedding reception of the bull rider and the sergeant,
freeway noise blocked out the vows, and all we had in common
with the other guests was fancy dress. Next day, Monday, nobody
wanted their job. A false summer haunted the parking lot with
light and dry wind, and by four we were in darkness with no
eclipse. The light came on, and someone young blasted music.
In came the graveyard shift and I was fast asleep.

AND THAT STAGE FRIGHT LURKING HERE

Your personage is tied to tubes like a trombonist. Hot-tempered bees
lay up amber inside critical air vents—they came to hear your pipes.
The sun rises through smoke in the eastern range, helicopters thrown
in this updraft like insects. It's a Pollyanna bauble of hope and good news
to get all your work done. You're counting down, and it's many more
binocular dreams before you wake. Could sound be less involved with food,
except for a call to eat? You assume the posture, recall the keys.

MEMORY RISES LIKE A FLAG

A delivery van brings morning, Soup for breakfast and a movie.
The sun gets people up and out, postcard-early. Skunk
in at dawn for the cat food. Left no card, fortunately.
The afternoon is night, snow on every field. It's light in the dark.
I teach my daughter guitar on someone's front steps.
I see a man drive urgently toward a gas station, closed.

I'D HAVE CHOSEN ANOTHER TOPIC

It was the pilot's view of streets. The shadow growing, more falling, then
nothing. Never saw a shadow, or map . . . so postcard. There you are at birth,
age twelve, after college, before marriage, heartsick and lonely without
a script. You cannot see beyond two hundred yards, flying along. You take
your glasses off and drive out of focus on Highway 10 through Coachella.
You see an orange-crate scooter leaning on a tree, more weeds. It makes you
an imposter to forget it. You pull your car to the side of the road and cry.

I FELT LIKE A MOVIE

The sun passes over a day without warmth like an old horse
staring at us from the far end of a corral, one back foot up,
ignoring hay. My resolve won't play the descending notes.
The old horse stands far off in the field in a drift to its haunches.
I give it, in minutes, a name and a place, sinking to my waist
as the feathery slope sleeps to shed me.

SCIENCE HONOR SOCIETY

I jump from the roof of my house to the dining room.
I place myself in the room as furniture, saying the pronouns
I, you, he on a cushion of air. It was another self, losing track
without permission. You can wander for months, an isolated body
after the dry-lake festival, patching the hole in the world, and die
with words. This is where you go with your health, into the jungle,
ambient light, every time awake, every object a parody of hauteur.
Once, I saw an old horse give up and die. That shocked me, that choice.

THE GIRL CHEERED

Gibberish, mine to yours—you're a flight risk. We don't misunderstand
your interest in clothes. The populist hero shouts into a deep cavern—
the monster gunship hovers above where beleaguered survivors of
oppression and destruction by evil machines have taken energetic
refuge. "Wake up." I despair the sequence, back out of an alley
with the Royce in reverse, the family following in the kettle car with
one gear forward. The nice people let us go down the center of the road
the last quarter-mile to my door. This would be a national park, green
bedroom communities vanishing in the distance.

YOU DREAM AGAINST FACT

Perhaps it's the rural mailbox, public places, grim's grim reminder
of here. You imagine your breath steam is from a hot spring. Fresh
people roll out of bed each century until the days are there when you're
not. You push out into the small cove of warm water remembering
your clean bedroom, tidy desk (for the first time in months), of
all things. You polish a skateboard with fluorescent chalk. Now you're
pure, a baby man who wanders in. A blue car turns into a Jack-in-the-Box.
Camus died in a car, unused train ticket in his pocket.

ABOUT RALPH

or Pittsburgh, and the boulevards we built wide . . .
It starts with a stop from thirst, a sleep in the woods, and
wondering about Ralph. He went nowhere on his journey, actually,
toward a polished glass globe with the power off, the static electricity
gone in a second, like you and your daily progress. Everyone stood
around to look. Best to look at me from the outside, at my skin in full
plumage. If I'd learned to say no, the clown would wear no tie.

TRIPLE CINEMASCOPE WIDE

So yellow with mustard, yellow, a newcomer color.
You didn't make this up: coastal ships with fire hoses
spraying each other in standoff, gold-laced water to a dark sea,
to a white sea, seaweed at your cuffs—this beach below
with clouds above, puffing thunder. The air flows in unobstructed,
each smell a version of salt and methane fish, and you, choking
in slow roil, your neighbor's wife topless on the sand.

NOW IT'S JUST LISTENING THROUGH A WALL

The sea is fallen aqua. The sky is yellow and the bay is quiet blue.
A memory of love passes through me. A cyclist with a spotlight on
his helmet, head down. I have trouble seeing in the dark, pedestrians
darting out, cars turning. I fall, and my strength goes inside. My time
was spent by others, observing me. I fall where I fall, through oak light
on light grass in the mud gutter and rise, or not, on some road,
both directions a puzzlement.

YOU OVERHEARD TALK OF YOUR INSTROSPECTION

The mirage of water on water turns cliffs of local islands into skyscrapers,
boats into buttes. These are marks from a man whose thirst goes beyond
the glass. My cup runneth afoot as if the seas burned off and coastal cities
became alpine. I'm better off in this skin. The dry sunlight freezes: You
splash like a meteor at sea. Your pool breeds mosquitoes. You pour your
life into its end, a volume with no capacity, appearing full. The black
cat escaped last night. It won't know its way home.

SMELL MY MOTHER'S GINGERBREAD

So long bone, hail brain . . . If anybody is looking for us,
tell them there is nothing but my hand. My colic and music
flow from a steady leaning and breathing. Nobody bothers
that domesticated crow. This is a job better done by daylight,
since sunsets fall on most with regret. I roll my program.
Swan Lake, beautiful, but I'm distracted by the ordinary look
of the oboist on the Jumbotron.

BLINK AT NIGHT, WOULD YOU?

All the foosball players kick at age-inappropriate bodies that roll past doors
holding paper funnels with oranges atop. Columns of arid smoke limn
the colloidal city, and now it's yours, throbbing with ridiculous caricatures
hidden in product design. With that, I adjust my chair and try to fool
the young by extolling vinyl. I'm crusted while sitting down to focus and
hear exile and the spike of sex with gritty teeth. Mask and headphones
to cancel the background noise, please. Art on the wall, lost skirts
and button-down pants. I watch a documentary on a tribe that tells
its old-timers they can't eat if they won't work.

WE'RE PAYING FOR PROTECTION BY UNIFORMED PEOPLE WHO ARE RUNNING FROM SOMETHING

The dog barked once. One end of me sticks out like a seal in waves.
Whomp! I push myself up the roof as a cartoon hulk and charge into
a candied park full of self-love, into a video game of me smashing bad guys,
texting passwords to enter rooms with spreadsheets, with graphs of my profile,
which pop up an ad for a car I drive off, escaping in canyons of keyboard
letters, a video through the narrow streets of St. Tropez.

DRY COMEDY!

No one really cracks it: a man next to the mouth of a small tiger shark,
dead on the sand. It looked like the shark ate the man, tilted to vertical.
Stroll with malt and dog till it's late and return to the night
where you hang like a bat above a stage with a chair, where you sit
telling stories like hunger writing home about cookies: arrested for
his debts, the man's daughter offered to substitute herself for her father.

THAT GOD IS FATHERLESS PROVES WE INVENTED HIM

The nation floats on a mattress, the masses roused for rebellion and battle.
There are fishermen sitting on lawn chairs, white roses in every rose bed
like cheap pearls, murder and wisdom in the same afternoon, the dousing
of cactus with a desert monsoon in a hose. Who kicks the gate, who leaves
for a bag of fall, few care. You're a blistering accessory on night-terrain in
the safe room. Making something besides lament, you are nodding.

FERNS GROW WHERE THE ENGINE USED TO BE,

azaleas in the trunk, passenger doors open to the parkway grass.
It's gossip, not poetry, getting back into the car on the old road, scuttled
for the crossing. You scream through traffic lights in the dark, pass
these other driveways of unknown sorrow whiskering the edge of
the one moon, and write this from the driver's seat, horns around you
blowing, black ivy grown back, ten years of quiet approaching.

PUNCH UP

Which brings me to the present. Like coffee and tree fall.
I turn the heater off to use the room for thought, within earshot.
Not hungry, getting smarter, dropping sound down the barbecue
chimney, I rediscover hearing. Like the jet passing above and a dove,
its roundness of room tone, or a faint radio. I hear them walking
and know a second thing with rations of coffee, so therefore arbitrary:
They'll soon be dead. If I trip and die, if old science and a god of Greeks
so erred, and we so err now in our science, and quiver trivial tortures . . .
The wool kings blinked in standoff. I'm filling out the check.

A SPY ON A DESTRUCTIVE CHASE, YOUR CAR, ONE OF TWENTY REBOUNDS

The world renews itself this way forever. This house will be
leaving the world. I stop the alarm clock before it rings. I run
my finger along the grout and trace a trolley route of those who died
not yet fully traveled. The calendar of courage called my week.
It's going to be a beautiful day. I'm going to be doing this for a long
time, pushing three kinds of trash cans: good, bad, and green.

I'VE DONE LITTLE WITH MY TIME BESIDES FANTASY

You pick through an old trunk: your rocket, your glove, your great-great
cousin's signed baseball. St. Louis Cardinals. The string goes back to
the sweet nuke, and you connected to the sun like a kite. You must admit,
the earth has a biblical setting, great blue infinity with wings, love, and animals!
—you one of them, still alive since day one. You follow the string, worm work
into a month of somethings: a picture of a friend now hobbled, with his kite
one inch tall, that flew and won the contest, whipping the air with popcorn tail.

A RAINWATER CISTERN FOR SHOWERS

I chose "jokes for sensual mouths." Your own flesh quarantined you
with malfunction. As if I hadn't lasted out my lost decade of trying
too hard. You have no better coat fit for survival. Like bugs on a blank
piece of paper skittering till they fall off, we should suffer, spill our worms
onto the table for others to swallow. I taste my battle with bugs with great
purpose. It's time to move the hedge from the middle of the street.

YOUR PERIODS ARE ELLIPSES

You left your effects behind in a simple country, single-file,
like elephants. The day's called off to plan for better times.
Propellers of all sizes spin like celebrating barbarians.
For forty years, never hitting the right word or leaving the park bench,
you watched contentment become error in the whirl and blade,
in productive toil. Happiness is revenge on misspent pleasure.
Show me no sign we ever fought a war; the old engine
of a biplane passing overhead tows its beach ad . . .

THE WEEKS AND FREEDOM FROM WEEKS

A pier reaches into the city for thoughtful walks. The leaking morning birds
bring blame for no reason. I'm eyes walking toward this with blood carried
a generation to this state of play, where I find manual guilt. I see ring after
ring of circle suburbs where no house shows hermitage, pressed on a sample
platter of how-not-to-do, picking crystals with tools. Pleasure craft tilt on
highways, and ordinary men and women lose hope when their grandpas
lie danceless, hollow to their own honey. Now, the starting over again.

THE WORLD IS ALWAYS TOO COOL

Our weeds and our stubborn cement: break the year in two.
I raise my sign. Mine says "fish," naming what I want.
I've flung ping-pong balls at the wind and landed a chip shot
in the neighbor's pond. I'm secure as an energetic monk. Here's our
seaplane on wheels rolled onto the beach beneath Diamond Head.
A little girl, well dressed with a crown of flowers, holds a hat box.
Here's your gaze, birds chattering in a dream mistaken for joy.

SENTENCES ARE TOOLS ASSEMBLED IN AIR

My insect sleeps and dreams the dream of bark. Old friends sway
in their wax while I unmask my camouflage and declare the dance
my costume. I watch this dark sea and moon acre, and feel shadows
in the dark. The skunk is black and white because it's seen by moonlight
only. Fair warning. Wet heads with flecks of rain come down the stairs
sharing M&Ms with strangers, warm but still asleep, fit for the unforeseen.
I'm intolerant toward gluttony, being munched on by time.

YOU CLOCK INTO THE CHOCOLATE SHOP

It's the deer hour when roads flip over, demanding calluses,
and fear overtakes you for your sins. Bottled in fuselages, you float
toward the soft land, race from the end of the world shoved into pipes
against the wind. By fiat all liquids must be sticky, including spit,
which would have shot us into the recreational river, had we lodged there.
This made rain easier, since droplets land as bushes, and you skate through
and past them, cut grass on the manicured battlefields and runners.

THE MODEST AWAKENING TO MY DISILLUSIONMENT

I dreamt this from an unnamed anxiety: A boy in shorts
sees a denuded tree. My mattress won't fit through the door.
It must be so. A landslide beside us as we sleep. A Mississippi
with smiling rafts and Ma & Pa mired, these who died young,
the drift of land under quilt of ice moss and surface pipes.
Ten years from now, the story is green. Consider the upside.

IF THE LEGLESS COULD MOVE ON SCISSORS

How can anyone say that? Our house beats yours in curb appeal.
Place a big spider on the table, then summarize: The whole house
up when it's so early? Adjust for trends, dismiss nothing, wait
for a crowd. The sting of snake, the cat's growl, everyone's running.
It's your party. You win the contest of milling around and mumbling.
Who needs to know you fell on the floor and landed on the carpenter's
unsanded chair pulled from the wall? The future? Now you don't like
that picture. Finally there's something to look at: a bird on a rooftop ledge.
People are happier than they were last year.

EVERYTHING ELSE IS THROWN AWAY

We are, right now, ready for next year in far-off groves, after the war
with elsewhere light. My grandparents saw the war factory here, sister
followed sister and they prayed in apartments as Catholics bubbling
beside Gypsies, followed blue through the spectrum of rain and music.
I stand back as though I were an undertaker speaking in code, as if music
were broadly understood. I'm vibrating faster. I'm someone's white noise.

THE UNKNOWN OF HIS GREAT OLD AGE

You nosed the egg across the lawn through the buckling sounds
of the day. This restart that sweeps you back to where you repeat
the right answers from a far-gone time, animals arresting each other . . .
this looks like the landing at the top of the back stairs where stacked
magazines, tied with string, pile like the cities you left. The worn geologies
of landscape echo lament of people never born, who never lived here.

PREDICTABLE AND ODORLESS

Your wife greets you with a good sleep behind her eyes, busy with invitations.
Something smells new. You fathered children here, urged faces in these pictures
to seek. You were famous inside this home. Your name is on degrees. Would you
have guessed despair would be so generous? You walk away slowly. Behind
you the promises to yourself and children who left you. Nothing left behind can
be kept from thieves, for no one's use, like things in a cardboard box. Trumpet
flowers all around, the car alarm goes off. The flag is your old school's.

KNOWING THEY (SLEW OF NEW) HAVE NO IDEA

They go back to school. I school. They surf. I make the boards and surf
my software. It's building up to something and won't stop, perhaps a music
that crosses to the blissful dead existence of now. Streets? They say we
don't need streets now. Carb man, dolphin man, elephant man. I catch
a life of breath held until they ask me if I am mute. My snow boots
turn to bolt up the sand from a rogue wave. Yonder fish—you see mouths.
We eat from wheels, lecture on mad cow, fish for subtexts.

BENIGN INDIFFERENCE

I break through headaches like stuntmen through smoke.
I'm the calm of frontier and war choices, peaking in citrus colors
where there are no longer groves. Thinking night was dark red,
I became, by floating upward, the graveyard, the string that holds my kite
to earth. I sit by the canyon and watch the healing insects float upward
in the evening air, eyed by birds, birds by hawks, myself by coming time,
counting days toward me in breaths, changing routes through monkey streets,
past naughty drunks tattooed on the boardwalk, or at the party where
the couple suddenly got married. I'll admit anything right now.

FOR THE RECORD, I'M A LITTLE BEAT−UP, BRUISED, HUNG−OVER

Put me behind a small job. If I were starting now, I'd start from anywhere.
I'm back here in a dry-grass weave that pays all tolls of waiting. Back
to work, many bred for duty and belonging. Does everyone sleep well
because I did? Open to a wall in the dark on pavement, a stripe, loud horn,
lights, grinding shriek of tire, eighteen-wheel trailer fishtailing over my head.

FELT PANIC WATCHING A FILM ABOUT PEOPLE WITH NO OPTIONS LEFT

The boys sit scared, hearing about the girl, the lake, the bypass of
moonlight for the first time. I lost a friend in that forest years ago and
now I've lost all my friends there. See the tall black tree and the miles
of knifing shore light? The reflection of a big white house bubbles
from the bottom of water. Those old battles are like yesterday's clouds.
We are ghosts in the morning. I laugh each time I wake.

HEAR A SUDDEN RUSTLE AND FEEL A THUD

Granddad took me in his car to school sometimes. He knew which way
to go. A left past two side streets, then a right confounded by bullies—
had my own troubles then, tried to put my lower teeth over my upper lip
to look fierce. I stand in my empty house and notice: on the street,
everyone wants in. I sharpen a pencil, open a door to the dark. I want
to fight them. That janitor has the classroom key. I have no red hair.

LISTS ARE AS SHORT AS MINISKIRTS

I've lost my understanding of regret, like a sense. Now
I get clean-up duty on the fragrant morning shift, trading backyard
death boxes for front-room tidiness. Everything looks great in the sunlight
by lunchtime. I enter a country hardware store with fishing tackle where
a child walks in wondering why the man selling lures devotes his time to this.

IT'S NO ACCIDENT

Try as you might, because we lasted, time will toss it. Responsibility
was our default as all countrymen walked blindfolded till circus day
beneath one magnificent landscape. It's a place we will not go by year's
end before a hot day in July in the dark. Hearing transitional music, glass
sees this like a false marina splayed over, while the trees are simply mute.
This summarizes my plot about the life that is over, given up to interruptions.
Glass knows already. Glass knows no gossip. I rise and wish to be left alone.

WHAT I SEE MIGHT BE BRICK, WHAT I HEAR IS CIVILIZATION

I've fallen into poor habits recently, gone back to live by eating, reading
Trollope, the evil numbers, not to suffer first breath of cool air as call
of calamity. Yodelers could. They would be looking for coins. And if I wrote
back to Lincoln, I would do as I'm told. Once, I told what I did. I do,
of course, eat, yearn, get whittled, sometimes win. Now I'm the clock,
calendar, custom, another year at my back . . . I roar at love:
flesh shot from a circus cannon!

THERE ISN'T

I stand in the hosed-off rotunda. The sweet past spreads with
the present's edge through my repetitions, adding soft wood
to root. The woman came to me as a tree, a hand to feel the old
good fortune and love beside it, eating spinning seed. She burned
tree to cook, like bandages, magenta clouds smoldering like moors
by a shore, and she, the one less broken.

GRIEF POSED WITH YOUNG LOVE DRESSED IN TAILS
AND FEATHERS

Sit back and watch the muscled shush of our right to a dignified cry.
I left with my flag's small pension: Let it be over, the war. To live
again, shuffling home across wide sand like an ancestor racing across
a new continent, a parched miner, mule dead, still alive . . .
I lift each object for its hidden cosmos, flat cardboard cutouts. I emerge
inside today's blood and harvest looking like a windshield after
a night-drive across the prairie, unhappy in my happiness that
I did not have this understanding when young.

LET ME ENTERTAIN ME

I chauffeur my story with tea to my room. See: a story with dogs.
My dog barked and rushed the TV screen, barking aggressively,
then ran under it in confusion. I'll make a sketch of time: a karate chopper,
as if he'd just come down with a fist and a shriek, very funny. Try to stop
and try not to move around. This pulls me in, strips time (decades of wasted
courtship) of its seeds without the old speculation of betterment. You've
pardoned the fools of summer and resumed. See the woman turning
left, that young man with a guitar?

"THE THIRD MAN, THE THIRD MAN"

I'm cloistered in a riot of cries. I've emptied my dust
like a cold Memorial Day barbecue. For the ditties
rocking my head with silent rattles, I grind my brain, dam up
my mouth against the centuries. I lived to tell the tale by cashing
everything out. I wished for drought, my bluff eroding,
ready to grow backward after a breath. I'm relieved from failure
since the inspectors died. I look into brick. I mean caution.
The cowards flee, leaving behind tiny hanging toys.

TO RECONSTRUCT THE MAN TAKES AN ACADEMY OF DAUGHTERS

The walls will stop talking when birds fly south. I find my self-discovered
self, nicely organized, larger for my years. I'll drop my pencil and sketch
my head. The long list of actions didn't make itself up; lawyers live in them
and laugh back at us. Then, the death of others, working till the end,
then a dog, being dog, meekly till the end. Green's green beams' versions
for everyone, free from influence. I hear the mules clanging pans—
my daughter is coming back from college. I hear stitching,
the high voice of a siren in dream-language, a squeaky gate,
and a bird making sense. I don't remember my despair, hard as I try.

I OWE THE RAIN MY DROUGHT

Here it comes again. I am tired of the door opening and closing.
I'm on a bluff under Mars, the closest it's been since the Ice Age.
I plow in good weather for the old man raging in his wars, sons
in their forties, tanned, riding red tractors, strong forearms
oozing honey, wives with young brutes about them, seed
longing for weed. To hear words would spoil the hollow mind.
Early is early. No one kills or harms a poet.

INTO THE LONG–TERM BABBLE THAT OUTLASTS US ALL

Lucky standby, you ran like a crab to the gate, knees stiff, the crab, your
beating heart. Next time you sleep, be more selective with your dreams.
Base them on the life awake. The door chimes only because people
like you in a stocking cap don't mention spring. You sit through the slow
hours ignoring them like furniture. Disappearing in a day means progress.
Your disease has found its patient, its unnamed protagonist. Your art is
your vice, admit it. You're fooling no one.

HOW CONVENIENT TO THINK A GOD IS RESPONSIBLE FOR EVERYTHING

I hold an almanac warning of a year without a summer.
The slips, the slumber, the sheets, the wee, the washer that
knocks, trash trucks that moan. The dripping arm of an alien sea
creature rises in the bay, watched by cliffs of witnesses who flee
with their machines. I'm not that old, but it reminds me of something,
a giant child with severe discipline. What is new is passing again.

THE LIVING AND DEAD HAVE EQUAL CHANCES OF SURVIVAL

You know that part: cactus and shiny quartz, heat-sweats all
morning. You see a plane taking off, an electron. I always mistake
the planes lining up to land for morning stars. I breathe air in
the presence of small fixed things. I've stifled the fervor and rifled the purge
and can be frank at last, my pictures in frames, my chaotic thoughts,
legs of screens, drum and harp, and coming storm. The locks riffed
the water heater's whistle. You see wax paper over glass, coffee
all over the fabric bag, improving its color.

THE NIGHT LIGHTS LIKE A WELDER'S SPARKS

A dark tree (eucalyptus) planted in the twenties, as tall as the view
is wide, ominous in the brittle ground—a juniper tree that aches in embrace
of a dead piñon downed by worms—a dark yard's construction zone along
the freeway. I made a circle (covered it) to be taken for a corral. Men plow
the good weather, no wind or cloud, the world born this way in its gasses.
There (now snow falls) will always be snow. I'm tired of preparing for death.

ALL YOU HAVE TO DO IS SHOW UP

All of us wave across the canyon from our stoves.
I pile broken pipes in a garage box thinking what accident
of child or worker will lift me in a mirror, unnoticed.
I'm cesarean and blue from the womb by first stab,
always seeing knives. I cross the continent, water cactus
pecked between thorns by elf owls, venomed creatures
crawling my back at night. The wind makes the glass hammer.
I see no reason to work this year, my father dying.

AHEAD OF THE COMPETITION

I walked into the room with my shirttail out. I shaved. I wandered
for years inside this fine isolation, emeritus of nothing. But now
I don't understand how they got here, doing the Civil War, doing
Gettysburg. I wait, better off in a silent, self-made froth with luxury
and invention on a bubble that holds, crossing off black things in black
scratches like Lucifer's books in sheets of snarls. Up early. The girl
I would have married in a second life had good news.

A DAY OF USEFUL TOIL

In the room there is a white table, the story of my skeleton
on an indoor barbecue, the story of my taste for meat and those
friends on a screen, the story of those eyes and ears. The windows
offer cold skin to the nippy belly. The room would be a different
room after a murder or marriage. The bountiful batteries on
the barbecue grill point opposite each other to power an unseen
motor. The propeller blows against my face, the tube of air
reviving the senses, says I'm right in this off place.

THE SCIENCE OF BLIND COMPETITIVENESS

You lift the car hatch with your elbow. You sit on an old couch
next to the ancient computer to listen. You pick at a banana next
to the stairs as the show starts, which includes the girl you
should have married (she should have married *you*) so unhappy
as she is now with the sudden divorce. All the phones ring, looking
for you. You have fallen on your back into the grass like daybeds.
You try to reset the start time to take a snapshot, battery dead.

AND NEXT, WHO KNOWS

I laughed again at the wet newspaper in the morning. During the night
it rained harder than I've ever heard it rain. It's an illusion we're solid,
because we're made of the same stuff. I'm a dancing old-timer holding
a twig with three leaves, smooth skinned, happy not to be log.
I'm finely centered in rows of corn, though movement requires
juking and harming plants. For fun, I spin in place, eyes open
to silos swinging by at the far end of a long passing train.

THAT WET WISH AGAIN

Then comes the fire where two counties' volunteers lose the barn.
A bale of your grass stands in the yard for sitting, for arrows,
to keep the trucks from rolling into the corn. Square dance on Friday.
Parcels from FedEx wait to be handed out. Jason's beer still left there.
Other bales pulled into bleachers while Rita's daughter learns to parallel park.
The milk of horses feeds trim foals, and I remember the floods and cowboy types
when gravel reached the fenders. I'm content two hours a day and call it lucky.

PULL A CHORD

Remember the image suspended in your hands,
the ball of the gearshift, the fiddleback dash,
the sun wiping out the image as the truck turns into the sun?
You view the faux-wood dashboard with a streak of sunrise
as fiction in fiction on the back of an old digital camera
someone left at a party. You only have photographs,
the past without permission. You said you could start over
like an imposter, forgetting the image will die with the battery.

IDLE TELEVISION, LOOSE ART INVOLVING NO ONE

You didn't think to write it down or net the digits like bees.
Dust the psyche. Bag it. What a little static will do will surprise.
Freely you send empty letters on the lick of stamp. You pull yourself
away suspended in delay from a balcony walk, no oldies on the radio
for twenty counties. You haven't become the car you drive. There you are,
a hybrid of cities headed for Japan, blind-gearing through weeks of fire
clouds. Your right mirror is misaligned. Blue smoke, flatbed breaking,
skids, chopping off your head, free (one exit to go) of paranoia.

EVERYWHERE AT ONCE

And here you are in a narrative setting, skin warm, on display,
symbol in a ritual, still asleep, reading from a book with blank pages.
You come bearded, full of joy, with fishing hat, beige coat, and shorts.
You unfold the best-to-come map, fabric containing a halcyon park
or resting place deserved, empty room and bare shelves, a fool's
move before the next emptiness of new shelves, all shelves.
Books make shelves. Books make people sleep in perfect pain.

HATCHERY OF IMPULSE SPEECH

I devalue each bliss and misfortune to an example and brick them
in the backseat. My hand walks my body, my mind walks my hand.
Largesse makes me fit until the timers start dating the hours. All is black
with electric logic haunting despair. This always makes me scratch and lift
bone, pull a Post-it to the trash and feel ahead. Little cells display lights
of a city made from different matter. The shadow world is ours. The copper
world, theirs. The lightning world, of itself, starts from a chosen nowhere.

ALL ROADS LEAD HERE

I lie on grass that fringes oak roads in winter, wander
into strip bars, looking for friends, where I see a conventional father
with two two-year-olds, a family strip bar open to the sidewalk, open
for lunch. The route here, mapped by a friend twenty-five years ago,
indicated no cliffs. I accept the same terms that started me out. Tomorrow,
I'll march to see for myself. I still hear music, the *klunk* of everyone's
noggin, windows blowing out, and common sense.

NEIGHBORHOOD WATCH

I walk unaware of shoes and retrace my steps. I walk discovering I'm not
wearing shoes. I pass the blue wall and ask in an upstairs fish restaurant
if they'd found any shoes. I can't change. I can't blame blankets
for troubled sleep. Made three mistakes today: walked through traffic,
crossed through hedges, drifted through backyards, too large for my years.
We'll fall through the floor onto our dreaming body and wake it. All's right
as I walk along the sand unencumbered, carrying my shoes.

FLASHLIGHT

If it's important, you will lose it. You go into a room lit by the earliest
gambit light, wearing a suit of feelings, have the day ripped and handed
back to you in small strips, two hours wide. You turned out the lights
and got everyone to shine flashlights on the wall. Eyes replied by waking
in the dark. It was the day before the planets fell, the day you said yes to heal
the broken sprinkler, the day life with dead friends was occasion for fine
thoughts, the day headlights veered into you warning of danger, the day
you saw turning from you before it ended.

WILL YOU EVER SUMMER IN PRAGUE?

The yellow velvet car drape, it's yours. The boy, the girl,
everything in rolling bags you can pull off the hill
down to the beach—the filling station, the diamond studs,
the doll river and signs. This lot goes back to Spain in a ship,
yes, from the cluttering storm where Cabrillo landed. He's back,
and we've whittled it down to this: A flock of liberated parrots
screech overhead. It's you that needs packing.

IT'S SUMMER AND HE'S STILL IN PRAGUE

I flick my headlights on high at a truck heading toward me.
The street is gold the sun stole. Fortunate greens allow me
to cruise all the way through town to pick up the drop.
A wheelbarrow of dust, wires, and pens, the gap left
behind in a move, and after that, my arrangement of objects—
the big truck brings new tomatoes—the dumpster nearby is full
of red glory and primal mash, reaching for example.

WHY IS THERE AN OCEAN IN MY BACKYARD?

My key ring has the key to the bowling alley. A paper sack
that once held concrete, blown here one storm, ages to ash.
I hear at regular intervals the heater, the trash truck up the hill
and, lately, the compulsive mockingbird lost in the treetops
like little electromagnetic pulses. I glimpse at the knee-high weeds,
the lawn frozen by an ocean, the blue and gentle current
forgotten in physics, as I wait for the house to get up.
I'll only make sense to me. I have so much me with time to explain.

I DIDN'T KNOW HOW TO TALK ABOUT THE SUNRISE

He chides each empty star, a forgotten local hero. He's back.
He mistook the chain on the bathroom counter for liquid,
did not see the river rise or hear echoes in the chassis made from
the same steel as bells. Birds in the foyer, his fate in black marks
on paper, he mails another empty package. In a safe-house garage
these packages stack like cubes of fever-dream. He leaves me behind
to ski down the paunch of a sleeping avalanche, sadly ominous.

TOIL IS HEAVEN

From the Phillips heads, massive tundra of police clover, cautiously,
even cleaving, you came. You lost yourself. Your version of the show
includes the girl eating fruit, the glass sliding door and a whoosh of quiet,
sharp rocks beneath you. The notch of all prizes is the flame beside
freeways, like it was your own invention: the traffic jam and fire.
It will be prisms and popping to my paying customers, fuming over
the nonresponse of the mass audience. Later come the gliders. If
you slept, you'd ride into town on a plumbing-fixture goat.

AND I NEED TO STOP

The brakes are soft on my car. It's Tuesday, and I haven't taken
it in. I can't go back from here to LA, to my trees, where my house
burned. Stocks of toothpaste in the bathroom, room by room. Buffeted
by wind and the dry yawn of morning space, the house was a porch
with a view stripped of its seats. No one knows or cares I'm a former
surgeon of trees, living the desert life, spelled by an acronym of clues.
I fell on the floor, found the balsa-wood pipe wrench. The nerve of
them, on our property without permission.

MY ART HAD NO STRAIGHT LINES, MY STRAIGHT LINES HAD NO ART

Early morning. Cars fill the lot in front of the supermarket.
You did one thing right and stuck with it while others electrocuted
themselves. Go figure. Funny how much happier you were with
the emptiness of postponement vs. the emptiness when work
was done. Everyone sees who kicks the gates, that you are
temporary, despite having no gun. Old age lasts fifty years.

MY WOODY CALLIGRAPHY AND WORDY CHOREOGRAPHY

My costume, my sensational downsized past, my dungarees, my
way west from Ohio, my main character, my breath, catching,
my vast lifeline, my policies in order, my wife, my program spindled again,
my friends, slow growth, clean shade, my practice, my product for asphalt,
my town through cartoon eyes, my sand houses, my gate between pasture
and drought, ennui as rain, earth's art, my bad habits, my political war and
avalanche, my new hardware, too prone to clipping by scooter, my
properly weighted luggage, and my heirs who will see, wonder over me.

THE WATER IS ACTUALLY COLD

The work of art stops our conversation about Camus. I confessed
I loved you and left it there. Your legs, crossed nicely below the knees,
Für Elise playing on the commercial for fish, cheek with *brune* hair,
young sees young as young. So art is a mess, ankle deep, transparent
fish in this murky layer grown silent for years. Flushed of notes,
I didn't realize that everyone just wanted to wake from a dream
of grief where the work of living begins. Death is easier than most
of our daily challenges because it is without consequences. I pass you
going east next to your chosen one.

I'M DEAD

Be pragmatic. Dam, count, trade. It's simple. Now for time, your spare time,
carry around signs. Pole or not, we all carry signs. Try the sign "for the living."
You're dead now and the other people, the other dead, only read the dead.
The living like to see things worked out for them, the surprises, the twists.
Simple. There you are, an invisible sign bobbing in the crowd, or flag staked
over a headlight pulling in front of the consulate, honoring the dead and
the unmet-not-yet-living, with this simple twist, I'm dead, then, with you.

NO ASSOCIATING MOBS

I hear raging in the twisted grove. Dust devils polish
the moon as shirts dance. The window's pleats of water-flow
wash the knockdown of dust. My family and I live on this
street. Nothing is safe but confidence, but the rest, in surreal
entertainment, moves out of town sealed in the past like an
organ in a jar. Now we won't fit into the crumbling room with
a plastic bucket of lint, react locally as if water were bees—

UNDERWRITER

I formally declare my rebellion. Here I sit, a five-billion-year-old science
experiment in randomness, aware of a fiery god who appears each morning.
Showmanship ends. I fall asleep and forget to take snapshots. I didn't write
letters. I turned and faced fifty dead souls with shaved heads. The dead lived.
As if the dead didn't think. I'm going into the barn for winter, with baby grain
bouncing down steel chutes to mother dirt, with lazy birds and shotgun blasts
and flocks turning like decisions in that morning light, while I cradle
mice in rags, dreaming of all the long legs in black soil.

THEY EITHER BUY YOU BECAUSE YOU'RE CUTE OR THEY BUY BARBIE

We met at the bottom of the stairs and stood for a time.
The street snapped like a sheet, then settled on its curbs, glittering
dust. I held your hand (you stared at children) the last time you hit this
low. It's the bounty days, they're cutting down our trees, the cathedral
trees. Behind the smell of pine, scorched landscape, there are things I can't
change. Stretch the line out far enough and you yourself will give up
or step out of the car into the passenger dust.

SO NOW YOU'RE LEFT WITH JUST YOUR ENEMIES

A small moth is boiled alive in hot coffee. Summer is standing
in the street, unlocking the car. I wish for another day to rest.
I'm finally at the end of my days. We are one of our father's sperm,
a cartoon hope in the head, mocking the light of the landscape in
the final decade of chance, an overflying contrail glowing, ears
plugged with honey . . . it's more nourishing to chew paper.

THAT'S APPLES TO FAST BY

But I never investigated. Fireworks and a bath for everyone!
A hero's wreck is national myth. You skip a meal. And here
you are, a hermit without army, to start over as a prizefighter,
on a three-wheeled recumbent with a yellow aerial, banking
against lavender, robbing time from your pockets. And then
the concourse, the oratory, carnality, oxygen, seven shouters
midsentence in a catlike glide. You stare at your shoe. You
stare at your corrected tactics. The same.

NEWS VANS, OUCH!

So the argument goes: Festooned the phone poles with ridiculous freedom,
tripped on old roots tilting up the sidewalk, cured our hubris like a quake
without a rumble. The redwoods here are large, but a lifetime's a poor way
to measure. Never sell America short. They're probably shorting you. But
I am worrying, and there you are waiting for the next thought that brings
me up to this moment. I invited my living friends to this long-forgotten
beginning of a story of neglect. The part of me you see is here.

ACKNOWLEDGMENTS

Thanks to editors of the following journals for publishing some of these pieces: "There Isn't" and "She Talks, He Talks" in *Adanna Literary Journal*; "Science Honor Society" in *North American Review*; and "I Met an Acrobat Who Said This Place Had a Nasty Room Roll," "The Prop Man Thought the Gun Was Fake," and "For the Record, I'm a Little Beat-Up, Bruised, Hung-Over" in *Poetry Bay*.

OTHER BOOKS FROM TUPELO PRESS

See our complete list at www.tupelopress.org